SHAMANIC JOURNEY

CONNECTING YOURSELF TO THE UNSEEN WORLD AROUND YOU

By: Conrad Keo

To receive the free guide "10 Easy Ways to Meditate Daily" and be informed of Conrad's newest books...

Sign up here - bit.ly/conradkeo

Copyright 2015 by Conrad Keo - All rights reserved.

This document is geared towards providing exact and reliable information in regards to the topic and issue covered. The publication is sold with the idea that the publisher is not required to render accounting, officially permitted, or otherwise, qualified services. If advice is necessary, legal or professional, a practiced individual in the profession should be ordered.

- From a Declaration of Principles which was accepted and approved equally by a Committee of the American Bar Association and a Committee of Publishers and Associations.

In no way is it legal to reproduce, duplicate, or transmit any part of this document in either electronic means or in printed format. Recording of this publication is strictly prohibited and any storage of this document is not allowed unless with written permission from the publisher. All rights reserved.

The information provided herein is stated to be truthful and consistent, in that any liability, in terms of inattention or otherwise, by any usage or abuse of any policies, processes, or directions contained within is the solitary and utter responsibility of the recipient reader. Under no circumstances will any legal responsibility or blame be held against the publisher for any reparation, damages, or monetary loss due to the information herein, either directly or indirectly.

Respective authors own all copyrights not held by the publisher.

The information herein is offered for informational purposes solely, and is universal as so. The presentation of the information is without contract or any type of guarantee assurance.

The trademarks that are used are without any consent, and the publication of the trademark is without permission or backing by the trademark owner. All trademarks and brands within this book are for clarifying purposes only and are the owned by the owners themselves, not affiliated with this document.

Why I wrote this book

We all have been touched by nature in some form one way or another. When you were young you could probably remember seeing squirrels dancing around on the ground inquisitively watching your every move.

Maybe taking a trip to your nearest forest will provide all the sounds and particularly the smells of the pines and abundance of trees. This immediately has a calming and refreshing sensation that reminds us of an everlasting bond with nature. Hopefully you have some favourite spots you visit frequently whenever you need to relax and get away from it all.

Just think about that fact. We find peace and increasing harmony the further we go into a natural landscape. We feel alive and at ease. This should remind us that this is the natural environment for mankind also. This is where we are from and should never forget it. If you really do feel at home here then also remember to treat it that way.

Why you should read this book

If you agree with any sentiment in the opening introduction then read on because there is a whole lot more to explore. This isn't a book just about the forests or animals and birds or the oceans and planets above us. It is about how we as humans are deeply connected to all of these and we should have a greater understanding of our unbreakable relationships with each and every one.

The shaman understood completely and was our guiding forefather along our journey of finding our true place on the earth. The shamanic ways and studies are still in abundance today if we choose to look into this fascinating world we are trying to leave behind. The ancient shamanic practices not only tell us why they were needed in the first place but why we should embrace them today because for most of us it has never been more important than where we are today to understand our place even as individuals.

The shamanic cultures nurtured their understandings of all the beings and life cycles provided in the natural world. From the incense of burning fallen tree bark to sustainable hunting and fishing nothing was wasted and everything had its rightful place including us. We still stare at the transfixing power of a simple campfire and marvel at the majestic night sky bursting with stars and celestial light. If we really learn to understand these evocative sounds and feelings once again we can truly sense nature and the cohabitating wild animals all around us. We should listen to them because we can still learn from them. They can remind us and show us where our true place is and the more we understand this harmony and delicate balance of nature the more we can call it spiritualism and pass it on to our children who deserve to be taught. After all it is already their world we need to educate them about. We should take on the role of the wild animals we can often hear at night and the lessons they show us and teach our own offspring all about our place with Mother Nature.

TABLE OF CONTENTS

CHAPTER 1. THE INNER SELF AND THE UNSEEN WORLD

CHAPTER 2. DEVELOPING YOUR CONNECTION

CHAPTER 3. THE EMERGENCE OF YOUR INNER SHAMAN

CHAPTER 4: THE TRUE MEANING OF SHAMANISM

CONCLUSION

Chapter 1: The Inner Self and the Unseen World

The general concept of finding our way to connect with nature is to first explore our inner self and learn as much about what really makes us tick before applying this knowledge to allow for the signs coming from nature to help show us the way further.

So first we must think about our inner self. This has been called spiritual intuition, divine mind or divinity and even spiritual intuition. These all refer to getting us to open up and recognize how we can find the innate power we have within to make connections with nature. Both New Age fads and the ancient practices know very well this is as much about spirituality as it is simply connecting with nature.

There are various techniques that can be taught and learned about the ways of approaching these realizations but the concept is roughly the same that is we all possess the power and insight inside to make a significant connection with nature and our trials through evolution. There are different descriptions and terminology stemming from the various techniques but the main point is to apply as much open mindedness whichever way you choose.

The World Of The Unseen

Once you make a start to opening your inner self then you can concentrate on finding the unseen world all around you. This will mean you can change your consciousness to be more open and in tune with the environment around you. Mankind has had the power to be influenced by nature for thousands of years. As far back as prehistoric times our ancestors could shift their consciousness to another state of being.

From there he could explore other realms, experience different beings and discover other energies. This knowledge has never been lost but it has just been buried deep within. A journey to your inner self to reclaim these ancient rites is a rewarding experience through a better understanding of self-awareness and appreciation of deeper imagination.

We are social animals and have developed higher social skills along the journey of evolution and we can now even think of the creation of the cosmos but do we do enough to think about our correct place within our small part of the celestial soup?

Although our animal cousins are also capable of thought and deep awareness we are probably the only species that has applied a coding system to spiritual concepts and practice ritual meetings and appoint priests and shaman etc. operating in religious buildings with congregations. We enjoy including social structures, music, art and architecture.

It is in fact true that our actual human spirituality lie in our animal feelings of connection. We have only extrapolated this level of being into creating the universally present elaborate forms of religion we have around us today. We should acknowledge and respect our fellow creatures and the spiritual awareness that have shown us the way and humans missing out on such connections are usually the ones that suffer emotional problems and a lesser form of basic mental health.

There are reports of humans succumbing to insanity from losing spiritual connections stemming from our natural matrix all around us. Mental illness is the evolutionary price mankind pays for having big brains and the inherent ability to abstract feelings.

They say there is a fine line between genius and insanity and it therefore would take a very special human to survive the onslaught of genius just as the same for an animal understanding any sort of concept of abstract. The incredibly long time it took man to evolve is testament to this delicate balance of our mental health.

We have come a long way from just animal instincts and a daily battle for survival. We are the only animal to have more than basic intuitive feelings. We can rationalize and quantify but this does not mean we should cut the link to our prehistoric skill set.

We can and should retain as close a link as possible to our past and we can now only do that through a clearer connection to nature and the animal world, the unseen world around us.

Chapter 2: Developing Your Connection

Does this sound familiar? You have a to-do list that seems to get bigger and bigger every day. You have an agenda and sometimes your meeting is about how to find more time. You have the latest cell phone, pager, organizer and tablet to remind you what you are doing all week. You spend half a day getting upgrades downloaded to make sure your apps are all current and then suddenly half the day is gone already. Where did your planner go wrong? Maybe you need another gadget to find the answer?

The thing with our modern world is that we are actually make our lives more complicated not easier. More toys means more things to go wrong. Okay, so you like all the latest gizmos and are a bit of a geek but did you realize that all this disappearing time means disappearing energy?

You may be happy in your techno cocoon and all is well until someone accidently cuts the power cable in the street and then you have nothing to do. Ever wondered what you might like to do during broadband downtime? (Assuming you have any). Do you think you don't care for anything outdoors because it's...well...outdoors? Is the outdoors for other people? Ever wondered if there is something outdoors that will appeal to you but you just don't know it yet?

Chances are there is a lot outside in the real world that will appeal to you. If you realized this then your to-do list would suddenly become much shorter as you discard all the modern time wasting things you just don't need. Think about how mankind thrived for thousands of years before electricity.

It is easy to turn the corner. Just get in tune with the awareness you have inside you. Notice things outside the window and look deeper into what is going on. It may not seem like it effects you but in some way it will. Learn to appreciate everything you see around you. Sights, sounds and smells should fill your senses and these will get stronger the further you go into nature. Once you have become aware of sensations around you, you should investigate further into the magical world of making connections with nature.

Chapter 3: The Emergence of Your Inner Shaman

The best person to teach you the ways of connecting with nature is someone with knowledge of shamanic ways. Shamans were the connection for ancient tribes to the outer worlds of nature and space. It was not so much how well a shaman could learn that decided who it would be in the village but who that person was. It was like the shamanic way of choosing who was right for the tribe shaman. It is a calling so to speak.

A shamanic journey ventures into what is called the Dreamtime. This is a place of spiritualism and symbolic gateways within the realms of our known world and that further place within nature. The natural laws of the universe are all around us and the shaman would understand this better that anyone and help explain this to the tribespeople.

The journey, although seeming like a trip form earth to the stars in the night sky, is actually more of a journey contained within. The journey can only start from within a person who is willing to open up inside and acknowledge the path that is available and laid out in front of them.

The shaman would conjure up the spirits of nature to get into this position of openness. It is known as shifting into another realm but it is just a question of throwing off your normal daily stance on life and letting yourself move into the spiritual world that is a constant cocoon all around you.

The shaman would summon these spiritual forces and help people journey into the next realm and it was powerful enough for people to achieve another state of consciousness entirely. Sometimes this could be achieved through attained a trance like state.

This would be done with ultimate trust in the shaman to help the journey be safe and completely relaxed. Sometimes this journey could be conducted under a deep sleep and dream like state.

The shaman may use bells and gongs and light rhythmical drums to help stimulate trance like environments to travel through. It was normal to use the sounds and smells of nature to help with this journey. Incense candles and sacrificial offerings could be burnt to help create the right atmosphere.

This is where you will most likely discover your spirit animal. This power animal can be your guide to encourage you and ask you to face inner fears and achieve spiritual goals that can influence you in your daily life. There is so much to learn but no two journeys may appear exactly the same. Perhaps you are aware of your spirit animal and want to discover further what this special relationship can do for you.

You may have researched ancestors that were also in tune with the spiritual world and you may be intrigued to retrace their steps and maybe picked up messages they have left behind for you. Either way moving into shamanic trance likeworld can be very personal and mean different things to different people but this unique experience should never be passed up if you get the chance to work with an experienced and knowledgeable shaman.

It is a very good thing to work with a real shamanic guide. You will get expert guidance into the ways of opening up to the spiritual world. It would be a good idea to be ready and prepared for this awakening because you can never tell exactly when the spirit will call us. It is important to know that this is exactly what you are experiencing and better still you can recognize the signs and symbols that are trying to get through to you.

This spiritual calling can come to any of us. When you think about it, you can safely assume that the exact same message came to your shaman a long time ago and they may have reacted with surprise in exactly the same way. This means that, like them, you must simply be open to the concept of spiritual messages being in waiting for you and you could make a very real connection and start your journey.

Not every shaman may have wanted to become one. They may have had no real notion of the coercive forces of nature being so strong that sometimes they would seek out the person rather than the other way around. It can often be this powerful and rather than fight it the individuals concerned may have been open to the idea the spirit world is asking to change their lives forever but always in a good way.

Imagine the scholars from the Old Testament that may have despised the radical new way of thinking called Christianity. What we would scarcely believe today must have happened at some time to some very learned men who had to adjust to a revolutionary new way going against their prior knowledge. We do know nature is all around us and we know how powerful forces of nature can be. We should also acknowledge that we came from a brand new planet out of the fire, water, and dust where life was first created.

Are you capable of being a shaman?

So what are the requirements for opening up to nature? Here are a few steps to act as a general guide.

Step 1 Conquering Inner Fears

Fear can be a terrible thing. It can halt you in your tracks and stop you from carrying on as normal. We become a different person under fear, sometimes to the extent of not being able to recognize ourselves. Fear makes us do rash and crazy things and we sometimes forget the logical or progressive way to look at the very problem facing us. When we fear the unknown this is an unfounded fear. It is borne out of ignorance and should be avoided. We can do this with knowledge and experience. Otherwise we are robbed of our personal power.

Why should we allow ourselves to have fear when this can be remedied by simply be open to learning and further understanding? Being fearful of something we do not understand is being oblivious to new challenges and experiences. This is not a true fear. True fear is standing up to something you know very well and understand its size and strength. This is where courage is needed.

Step 2 Develop your Presence through Courage

This means use your courage to accept a challenge and use the inner strength within you to triumph over your latest adversity. This is not really steeling yourself to break out of a dark alley or take on an attacker but to face who you are as a person and have the courage to question your fate. Ask yourself if you are ready and willing to open up and challenge everything you know. It is about having the courage to put off worrying about tomorrow and disregard all your previous experience to embrace the now.

STEP 3 CHANGE YOUR STORY

We all have stories. Our lives become a collection of stories containing the best bits we remember and try to forget the least happy times. Either way we use these past stories as a yardstick to judge our present predicaments and future options. This is not always the most reliable way to go. What if we are basing our conclusions on an error in our data base?

The way of nature taught through shamanic ideologies is to only live for the moment. To take in every single thought and sensation that is currently happening to us. This way we don't have to recall hazy information or let emotions ruin our heads.

We can logically and instinctively surmise all that we see hear and feel and go from one scene to the next making the best of every situation. Remember how as children everything we do is trial and error during that brief moment? Why not live our lives like that. Enjoy every second of the good things we surround ourselves in and have the courage to face the bad things there and then every time. No regrets, no grudges held and no guilt to eat away at us.

STEP 4 BE THE CENTER OF YOUR POWERS

This means caring for oneself on different levels. Look out for yourself as a partner would. Reward yourself with doing well. Be happy with yourself like a marriage. Don't go to bed on an unsatisfactory note. Deal with your issues and make your improvements. Realize you are only cheating yourself on life's journey if you don't.

If you don't put your own house in order you will lose the skill to see the good housekeeping in others. This is a bad place to arrive at. Your judgment will become cloudy this way. If you can't feel satisfied with yourself that you are trying your best you will not reciprocate with others.

Have good self esteem and always be willing to improve yourself.

STEP 5 PATTERN FINDING

Pattern finding is taking one's corrective skills to the next level. If things are still going wrong although you feel you are doing everything to your best ability then it is time to fine comb your patterns in life and look for any ripples. Follow your life path diligently and look for disturbances in your life patterns. The tiniest ripple could be the clue to your less than obvious problem.

STEP 6 BE A MODEL

Again, this is another step up the ladder of personal achievements. If you have ironed out your most delicate problems you can be a model or inspiration to others. You can now lend a hand and be a shining example to those further down the road trying to catch up.

This is not about ego but being satisfied with your achievements even in the face of scorn or jealousy. You don't need to rub people's noses in their criticism of you as this is bad form but be pleased you can rise above it and not need to stoop so low.

Step 7 Mentoring

If you have done well as a model and are happy you can stay focused and productive above any negativity then you may well have arrived at the stage of being a natural mentor for others.

Once you have learned the rituals of shamanic ways and have found true peace with who you are and how you connect with the spirit of the wild then this step may now be for you.

If you're ready to share your energy and knowledge and can point people in the right direction to find their connections with nature then you may be ready to be a shaman. You do not need to be an expert on all the spirit animals and everything there is to know because there is too much for any one person, but if you have learned enough about yourself and know how to bring this out in others you may be on the threshold of this incredible end to the journey.

CHAPTER 4: The TRUE MEANING of Shamanism

The official line of a shaman's capabilities is centered on one who can move between altered states of consciousness. Now this doesn't have to mean it is akin to a witch doctor using tribal medicines to go into a drugged trance but an individual who has such a clear understanding of their identity and the place they should fit amongst everything around them that they can see many alternate ways of looking at the same point in time.

The word shaman actually comes from Siberia and it literally means someone who could see in the dark. This has a better comparison to our witch doctor friend. A shaman is therefore a leader and inspirational character for others. This can be far reaching as their duties include flushing out bad spirits and dark forces that may have a grip on an unsuspecting individual.

The beauty of the spiritualism a shaman can call on is the fact that they don't use magic or hocus pocus or any unnatural but will use their spiritual insight in to doing not much more than restoring the natural balance of a person or situation. The shaman has learned such an understanding of the natural world that they have this foresight to see how balance can be restored. This is nothing to fear but to admire.

THE WORLD OF THE SHAMAN

Shamanism is one of the oldest forms of healing on the planet which alone commands a very high level of respect. There are records of shaman like tribesmen in nearly every early culture during our evolution and this goes all around the planet. This has never been fully explained.

Throughout these diverse and unrelated original cultures, the shaman was adept at retrieving missing parts from a troubled person's soul. They could restore the connection to their spirit animal so they could receive guidance once again.

Shamanism is still going strong today and is testament to the incredible journey some shaman make. Sometimes a shaman must delve into the underworld to find help and guidance for the souls living above it. This can be very taxing on a shaman and they must remain fit strong and healthy and ready to give their all every time.

It is easy to see how silly the modern New Age fads have tried to sell shamanism as something that can be learned on a short decimated course in the wilderness. The journey of a shaman is actually very personal and different for each practitioner. It is not easy for them to teach the ways that have been handed to them sometimes unintentionally.

The first thing a shaman may admit is that true energy flows through all of us so we all have the potential to become a shaman but only a very few will learn how to read the signs and symbols correctly. These energies can come easily but leave us easily if not honed into a reliable recognition. Many people will not have the forthright dedication to learn the complex messages of shamanism. It takes a special person who is willing to give up their previous life and that is just for starters.

It is more correct to explain that a shaman learns how to adapt to everything around them rather than become an anointed one that holds the power to life.

A common analogy is like a swimming pool full of people. Some bodies create waves and displace more water than others but someone sensitive to these ripples, like a shaman, learns the ebb and flow of the water around each person. They adapt and learn lessons, *not* give lessons. A shaman will teach how balance is important but the individual must face up to what is causing the imbalances.

A shaman does not become all powerful and mighty but quite the opposite. They will learn how to bend and strengthen their energies until almost the breaking point to retain their connection to their knowledge but never break the bond.

Some students ask to learn shamanism to empower themselves and become instantly stronger or more wise, but a real shaman is more likely to explain that everywhere are power lines so sometimes many walks are needed to find power lines to fix broken connections and establish a lost energy source. A shaman will therefore contemplate very carefully the appropriate course of action and being powerful is often the last resort to a problem.

A true shaman will realize that every action has a reaction somewhere else so fixing one problem for a student may cause a ripple for somebody else. The shaman therefore fully respects the subtle balances of life and embraces the eternal sacrifices that are made in the natural world every single day.

How Do you Know if you Are a Shaman?

This is the most common question coming from all students of shamanism. How do you know?

Most shamans will probably answer that they themselves are still learning and will always be a form of student. There is no easy answer of course, but, it is often noticeable that a shaman may have had a traumatic or unusual event in their formative years. Perhaps a difficult birth or traumatic accident when still young may have set their mind on a different path compared to those around them. They may have seen people's perception as something inaccurate and decided before realizing it that they were different and this was likely to last for their life time.

Sometimes traumatic events can unlock subconscious parts in our psyche where a view into the psychic world may have occurred. This is necessarily a return trip to hell's fires but at least a slight shift may have occurred whereby the youngster is made aware that they have missed something important from the acculturation process. They may realize even then that they don't quite fit in.

When this alternative experience is met with mistrust or even hostility the unlucky recipient may get a twisted view of their abilities and develop psychological problems even to the level of being schizophrenic. Sometimes the strong energies that are skillfully tapped by a capable shaman may come too soon in life for young minds that they simply can't handle the raw mental power manifesting in their minds. Often these youngsters are given up by society far too early.

The early civilizations were not as harsh on these 'problem' youths as they could be taken to the shaman of another tribe for treatment. All was not lost in many cases and occasionally a shaman would pick them out for proper training and interrogation of their skills. Because it is a science not easily understood there have been many stories of students with potential being discarded and misunderstood by the entire society.

There is a famous story in India of a young woman. She was labelled as crippled, blind, retarded and delinquent as a child. In an ultra-modern society she would have been thrown on the social scrap heap. As it was she went through many institutions until her subconscious mind under interview started making prophetic messages for scholars to apply a wider mind to understand. Psychiatrists spent years trying to understand her delusional ranting until it was suggested these were shamanic messages coming from a special place deep inside her.

Over time she examined them until it became clear she had a special message for those that could hear it. She received hospitable treatment and was allowed to develop her understanding of these messages until she could make sense of them. Over the years she recovered her sight and physique and became very sane to the degree she underwent shamanic training and now teaches others. Tribal leaders firmly believe shamanism is based on destiny for the individuals concerned.

SIGNS SHOWN IN YOUR PERSONALITY ARE:

1. When you were a child, did you feel the urge to go into the wild alone for long periods and maybe spend nights there? This is a typical sign of a shamanic calling.

2. As a child, were you a loner? Were you considered eccentric or "different"?

3. As a child or grown-up, Have you seen, glimpses of the future? Or had repeated cases of verifiable déjà-vu?

4. Have you ever shown any power to cure illness or to relieve physical pains?

5. Have you ever seen ghosts or UFOs or felt that some Spirits have contacted you in some way?

6. Have you encountered the same animal several times in different dreams? Or have you repeatedly encountered the same teacher figure such as a wise and authoritative man or woman?

7. Have you ever had several similar dreams that predicted the future or that clearly showed present or past events you weren't aware of, but you could verify later?

8. Do you often have vivid or uncommon dreams? This means that your soul is attracted by the other Reality and it may be an indication of shamanic calling.

9. In this ordinary reality, have you ever met with the same animals many times, possibly in unusual ways?

10. Do you currently have the urge to learn how to become a shaman?

These are normally one most reliable marks of a shamanic calling, especially if you don't realize the motive of it and your urge is very pressing.

Books from Conrad Keo and Totem Guides

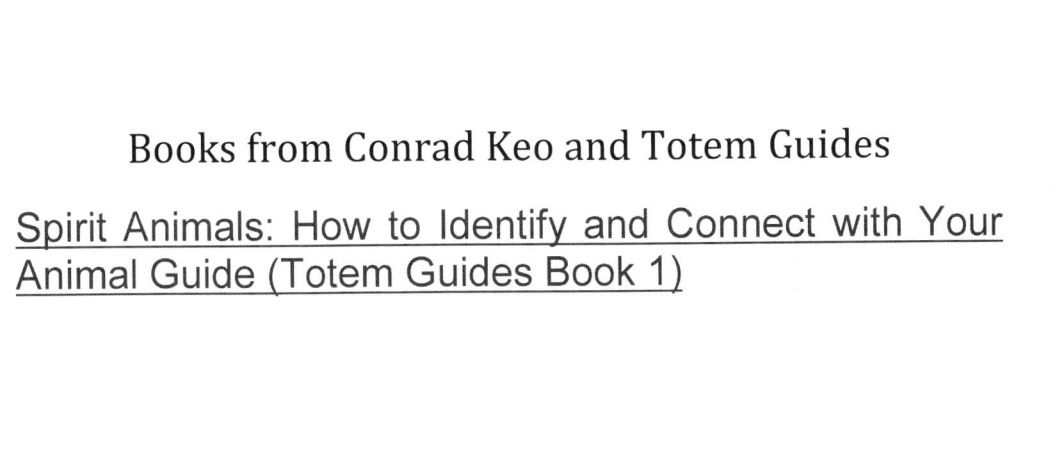

<u>Spirit Animals: How to Identify and Connect with Your Animal Guide (Totem Guides Book 1)</u>

Conclusion

As you can see, the ways of the shaman are steeped in history and deep connections with nature. In order to fully understand them, one must place themselves in a position to hear, see, and be willing to understand. Without these basic skills, trying to learn shamanic rituals and techniques will be irrelevant.

The whole purpose of the shamanic beliefs and sciences is to pave the way and make easier a journey. This journey will be spiritual and extremely personal for the undertaker. There is no easy telling where the journey changes from a personal experience within until reaching the outer, natural world.

Made in the USA
Middletown, DE
14 March 2015